KRISHNAMURTI

Praise for *Krishnamurti: Two Birds on One Tree*

"This small book is going to be cherished for many long years to come; its quiet, whispery resonances have a teasing quality to them that would warm the heart of any teacher or seeker. It is a sort of dialogue between Krishna and Arjuna, a dialogue that creates music and mirth, but the answers only whirl in the wind."

"Krishnamurti, as he himself said, is not the Answer. But he is the Interrogation. Ravi Ravindra succeeds in presenting that man whose life remains a constant challenge to our times—and helps the reader continue the search. It is not a biography of K. It is a splendid presentation of a living example of the constitutive quest of the human condition."

"I am very pleased you will be releasing this well-written book during the Krishnamurti Birth Centenary year."

KRISHNAMURTI

Two Birds On One Tree

RAVI RAVINDRA

QUEST BOOKS

Wheaton, IL U.S.A./Madras, India/London, England

The Theosophical Publishing House
P.O. Box 270
Wheaton, IL 60189-0270

A publication of the Theosophical Publishing House,
a department of the Theosophical Society in America.

*This publication made possible with
the assistance of the Kern Foundation*

Library of Congress Cataloging-in-Publication Data

Ravindra, Ravi.
   Krishnamurti : two birds on one tree / Ravi Ravindra.
       p.   cm.
   "Quest books."
   Includes bibliographical references and index.
   ISBN 0–8356–0718–6
   1. Krishnamurti, J. (Jiddu), 1895–1986.   I. Title
B5134.K754R38   1995
181' . 4--dc20   94-37859
                                                      CIP

   9 8 7 6 5 4 3 2 1 * 95 96 97 98 99

This edition is printed on acid-free paper that meets the
American National Standards Institute Z39.48 Standard

To
Krishnaji
for embodying
an immense stillness

CONTENTS

Two birds, inseparable companions, are perched on the same tree: one eats the sweet fruit and the other looks on without eating.

Rig Veda (I.164.20)

ACKNOWLEDGMENTS

Paul Kasdan, Steve Kay and Priscilla Murray were very helpful in the editorial and computer work. Without them this little volume would not have been published.

An earlier version of "Letter to J. Krishnamurti" was published by the Traditional Studies Press in *A Journal of Our Time* (Vol. 1, 1977) and was reprinted in S. Patwardhan and P. Jayakar, eds., *Within the Mind: On J. Krishnamurti* (Madras, India: Krishnamurti Foundation, 1982).

An earlier version of "The Mill and the Mill-pond" was published in *The American Theosophist* (Fall, 1986).

A slightly different version of "J. Krishnamurti: Traveler in a Pathless Land" is to be published in a book devoted to the contemporary flowering of Hindu spirituality, edited by K. R. Sundararajan, as Vol. 7 of *World Spirituality: An Encyclopedic History of Religious Quest* (New York: Crossroad Publishers, 1995).

The permission and courtesy of these journals and publishers is gratefully acknowledged.

FOREWORD

Jiddu Krishnamurti was one of the most re-markable human beings of our age. En-dowed with an extremely sensitive body and mind, he was often in contact with very high and subtle spiritual energies. His utterances in these high states had a quality of revelation because of their profundity and directness.

But Krishnamurti was also a man of his times. He was a product of his cultural upbringing; his early education and significant events in his childhood and youth left a mark on his psyche and colored his remarks and criticisms. As Ravindra says in one of the essays collected here,

It was as if he [Krishnamurti] had two distinct parts. His deep spiritual essence could soar without effort like an angel in the clear skies of Truth. When he spoke from that part, it was as if the heavenly choir were singing. The listener felt blessed and in total accord. Then there was the relatively superficial personality, formed by his personal history and his struggles to be free of spiritual tyranny. This part was born of conditioning and not of insight. When it took over, it was like the discordant note introduced by the uninvited thirteenth fairy in the tale of Sleeping Beauty.

Still, Krishnamurti was remarkably free of physical and psychological possessions and accumulations. His own deep inquiry, and his insistence on freedom from external authority, inspired in many who came in contact with him an independent search into the nature of human existence and its potential.

Ravi Ravindra, born and brought up in India, has lived in the Western world for more than three decades. Trained in the sciences, his own spiritual search has led him to a wide ranging study of metaphysics and spirituality, Eastern as well as Western. He met Krishnamurti, both formally and informally, many times over a period of twenty years in India, England and in Ojai, California. There were intense conversations between them, sometimes in small groups and sometimes just by themselves. They met over friendly meals, and there were many quiet walks together. Ravindra was always welcome at his table, in his seminars and in his company. In their dialogues, which went from insight to insight, Ravindra was respectful but independent—listening and questioning. Krishnamurti, like all truly great teachers, was less interested in being right and more in discovering the truth. In some of their conversations Ravindra would persist from his own clarity of thought and perception, and Krishnamurti would say, "Yes, you are right; don't let me say that again."

The three pieces selected here were written by Ravindra from different perspectives and for different purposes. They range in style and content from a personal and anecdotal account to an academic essay. All of these writings reveal an engagement of serious minds inquiring into the nature of reality, including the nature of the extraordinary intelligence operating through Krishnamurti.

PAUL KASDAN, STEVE KAY
and PRISCILLA MURRAY

Intelligence can only be where there is love and compassion. Compassion can never exist where the brain is conditioned or has an anchorage.

Love is: dying every day. Love is not memory, love is not thought. Love is not a thing that continues as duration in time. And, through observation, one must die to the continuity of everything. Then there is love; and with love there comes creation.

J. Krishnamurti

LETTER TO J. KRISHNAMURTI

It is precisely because I hear your call that I wish to write to you. The last time I heard you speak, I was once more convinced that this planet is blessed because Krishnamurti walks on it. This feeling adds to my urgency in writing to you. I can foresee the loss there will be when you are no longer here, corporeally visible, radiating palpable energy. Even though any one of us comes close to you at our own peril and must take the risk of being burned, something in your words encourages us to approach you.

I wish, first of all, to say something arising out of our shared cultural and racial history. It is perhaps owing to this common ground that I sometimes fancy I could be your younger brother. In the vast history and mythology of our land, there has been a continual outpouring of spiritual greatness. Maybe this is the special calling and genius of the land of the Bharatas. In my view, you, Krishnamurti, stand foremost among the living bearers of this greatness. In your life and your words you have expressed, perhaps more strongly than anyone else, the need for freedom—from tradition, from history and from teachers. And yet you seem somehow bound by our tradition's long sundering of the orders of time and eternity.

I sense a distortion here which I hope you will help me reappraise. The death of Krishna, when the present age of Kali is said to have begun, marks a radical discontinuity, monumental in its consequences, in the vision of the greatest of our seers. Since that time scarcely any among them—in marked contrast to those of earlier ages—have honored the demands of the world of time simultaneously with the demands of the world of Eternal Intelligence.

The first time I heard you speak was in a public place in India, not far from an exhibition of armaments captured in a recent war. The exhibition, designed to feed the euphoria of a claimed victory, took place near the center of political power in our country. There you sat, physically frail, a spiritual giant.

You inveighed against the hypocrisy and stupidity of our rulers with such moral authority that, for a few moments, my heart cherished the hope of a new age dawning in our land, which has been impoverished for a millennium by barbarians who considered winning the world more important than wooing the Spirit.

We had, no doubt, prepared our own ruin. When one of our greatest sons, Gautama Buddha, having conquered the higher kingdom, did not see fit to rule the lower, our later troubles should have been foreseen. From that time onwards, our saints have not been heroes, and our heroes have not been wise. If we had ceased to respond to the demands of our spiritual destiny, there would have been no reason for our continued existence. But what happened was that we did not give the world its due, and the world took vengeance, imperiling our very purpose.

There was a time when our sages married, raised children, fought battles and ruled kingdoms. What change occurred at the turning of the ages? For a long time our culture has not felt that this world could be spiritualized, or that an engagement with it could provide an opportunity for the honing of our instruments of perception to delight in the Spirit. We have behaved as if the world of time and space were a mistake, an unholy illusion, as if freedom consisted in escaping from it by retracting our senses and turning our minds wholly inwards.

I know this is not what you yourself say or do. Nevertheless, the division you make between what is of time and what is timeless has, historically, always led to a devaluation of the world, often followed by a reaction of excessive valuation. My question is, what cosmic necessity, in the scheme of things, makes this duality irreconcilable? Why is it that the two yearnings of my soul—seeking after timeless truth and a passionate involvement with the world—should be in contradiction? Could it not be that the fact of this dual yearning is our opportunity? Might it not even define our human task and place in the universal scheme?

I am now convinced that the resolution of my difficulties is not to be found in discussion or in doctrine, or in any other manifestation of thought. You have often pointed this out. If what is needed is an internal reordering which might make a larger vision possible, how am I to prepare myself for this? Is it solely a matter of grace? Can my thought or body in any way help?

Something in me knows you are right when you say truth is a pathless land. I know my own tendency to imagine that if I were to do certain good things, use certain right formulas, follow certain wise teachers, I should be enlightened and free. In spite of my intermittent wish and hope to the contrary, this much is clear to me: Truth cannot be achieved; there is no path which can lead to It in any determinant manner.

Does this have to mean that there are no models, injunctions or traditions which could influence a person—or even a whole culture—in the right direction? I am what I am, in confusion and conflict, only occasionally in search of order. Is it not possible for me to try to live in a manner that will orient me towards the Truth? Will the description of this manner of living not be a teaching? Does the teacher not, in fact, help? It seems to me that this process of preparation takes place in time. The question, then, is not how to escape the mind or the body or time or the world, but rather how to find their right use and place.

I sense something fundamental here. You speak about freedom from fear, from thought and from time. Freedom is only a rare and fleeting presence in my inner and outer world. For me, to be aware of what is, is to be aware of inner slavery, anxiety and vanity. Where can I begin if not from where I am? What I need is to learn how to channel my life energy into a saner mode of existence. Your immediate presence has sometimes refreshed my parched soul like a flash flood. But I need to begin to build a reservoir for a steady irrigation.

You have said that the everlasting is not eternal, and that an endless continuation in time does not lead to timeless freedom. But can anything in the realm of time resist the thunderbolt from above? Should we not expect that even the darkest recesses of our mind and of our society have the possibility of being reoriented? They also exist and are part of what is. Perhaps their energy comes from the same source which illumines our highest parts. In that case, no person can be wholly without some saving grace. Is what we need not so much to cease doing what we are doing, as to inform our present activities with awareness?

Perhaps our tradition's radical separation of time and eternity has severed us from a root source of vital energy. It puzzles me that in the land of Shiva and Krishna our spirituality has become so pious and meek. We seem to have become obsessed with a pure white light to the exclusion of all the exuberant colors. Our men have been domesticated and no longer roam as the wild rhinoceros. Nowadays, when one of us is blessed with the opening of the third eye, he does not go riding the bull Nandi, accompanied by his ruffian friends, to wed the mountain woman, Parvati, who will produce virile sons. It takes a robust holy scandal of a man to do that. We have become too tame, too proper, too other-worldly. How can we stand with Shiva, at the eternal still point in the circle of time, engaged in the rhythmic dance of life?

I wish to return to the question of taking "time" seriously and, along with it, "history" and "thought." When you say that thought breeds fear, I can understand that many fears are created and sustained by thought. But does thought always produce fear? Are there no fears which arise independently of thought? Perhaps what I am doing is analyzing.

I once heard you say to a large crowd, "Analysis is paralysis." I was aware then of the wholeness of your vision and of the possibility of an understanding more profound than analysis. But a year later, meeting a young man who quoted your remark as a slogan but could not hold a clear thought even for a few seconds about quite ordinary things, I was struck by the terror of what your subtle whispers can lead to in the hands of unprepared and undisciplined people.

You so often talk about real observation in which the observer and the observed are no longer separated from each other. Yet, clearly, you and I and a tree are distinct from each other; if in nothing else, at least in the spaces we occupy. What perspective is it in which the obvious particularities become insignificant and disappear? The feeling that I am, when present during perception, seems to anchor my fluctuating attention and connect me with what I observe, without eliminating my individuality. Does that imply that what distinguishes me from other beings and objects is less a part of myself than what unites me?

The reason I say all this to you is that you seem to be almost alone in our land in your concern with being aware of what is, rather than imagining what could be or should be. What is really important about you is that you are a free man—partly perhaps owing to the Indian tradition and partly, no doubt, in spite of it. In any case, you have the enormous spiritual power necessary to bring about a radical reorientation of a tradition. This, however, seems to require not only the vision of timeless freedom but also a participation in the joys and sorrows of this world and a knowledge of her laws. What is a human being if not a field of interaction between time and eternity?

What you have been saying for half a century strikes a responsive chord; yet to my understanding, it appears partial and incomplete. It seems to ignore time, change and becoming. I suspect it is my own anxiety that impels me to ask for a track in a pathless land, and for a process that will produce uncaused freedom. Nevertheless, something in me does not let go; and I am not sure whether this is my weakness or my strength. I am troubled because I do not know how to

reconcile the call I hear from your distant shore
with the realities where I am. It is clear that a
bridge cannot be built from here to There. But
can it be built from There to here?

With gratitude and affection,
RAVI RAVINDRA
1977

There is another art, which is the art of observation, the art of seeing. When you read the book which is yourself, there is not you and the book. There is not the reader and the book separate from you. The book is you.

Then you must also know what meditation is, what it is to have a very still, a very quiet mind. And it is only such a mind that can know the real religious mind. And without the religious mind, without that feeling, life is like a flower that has no fragrance, a river bed that has never known the rippling waters over it, it is like the earth that has never grown a tree, a bush, a flower.

When we consider what meditation is, I think one of the first things is the quietness of the body. A quietness that is not enforced, sought after. I do not know if you have noticed a tree blowing in the wind and the same tree in the evening when the sun has set? It is quiet. In the same way, can the body be quiet, naturally, normally, healthily?

J. Krishnamurti

TRAVELER IN A PATHLESS LAND

Truth is a pathless land, and you cannot approach it by any path whatsoever, by any religion, by any sect.

Because I am free, unconditioned, whole, not the part, not the relative, but the whole Truth that is eternal, I desire those who seek to understand me to be free, not to make out of me a cage which will become a religion, a sect. Rather should they be free from all fears—from the fear of religion, from the fear of salvation, from the fear of spirituality, from the fear of love, from the fear of death, from the fear of life itself.

For two years I have been thinking about this, slowly, carefully, patiently, and I have now decided to disband the Order, as I happen to be its Head. You can form other organizations and expect someone else. With that

I am not concerned, nor with creating new cages, new decorations for those cages. My only concern is to set men absolutely, uncondition- ally free. [1]

Thus on August 2, 1929, at the age of thirty- four, Jiddu Krishnamurti announced his great renunciation. He dissolved the Order of the Star, an international organization specially created for him by the leaders of the Theo- sophical Society, who had heralded him as the vehicle of the coming Messiah. Soon after- ward, Krishnamurti dissociated himself from the activities of the Society, although it is not clear whether he ever formally resigned from it. He wished to break away completely from the in- fluence of those who had sought to mold him and to confine him within a traditional messi- anic role.

Jiddu Krishnamurti was born on May 11, 1895, the eighth child of a Telugu Brahmin petty official, in Madanapalle, a small town in Andhra Pradesh, India. Before he was born, his mother, an unusual and sensitive woman, had a premonition that he was to be remark- able in some way. A renowned astrologer who cast the boy's horoscope was convinced that Krishna—as he was called as a child—would be a very great man indeed. The astrologer held to this conviction even when, to his father's great disappointment, Krishna turned out to be vague and dreamy and made little progress in his studies. From early childhood he was inclined to be religious, although he also had an aptitude for mechanical things. Generous by nature, he would often return from school having given away his pencil or slate or notebook to some poor child who could not afford to buy one. After his mother died, when he was ten, it became evident that he was endowed with clairvoyance and other special powers, for he often saw her after her death.

When Krishna's father, a Theosophist, retired, he moved with four of his sons to the Theosophical Society's headquarters at Adyar. It was there one day in 1909 that C.W. Leadbeater, a leader of the Theosophical Society who was considered a great occultist, discovered Krishna playing on the beach. Leadbeater was struck by Krishna's aura which he said was the most wonderful he had ever seen and which was without a particle of selfishness. He was convinced that Krishnamurti was to be the vehicle of Lord Maitreya, the coming World Teacher. Annie Besant, president of the Society, shared his conviction.[2] In order to prepare the body and the mind of Krishnamurti to serve as the proper vehicle for Lord Maitreya, Leadbeater and Besant took over the protection, care and education of Krishna and also of his beloved younger brother, Nitya.

In 1910, their father transferred the legal guardianship of Krishna and Nitya to Mrs. Besant. Later he changed his mind and launched upon litigation that dragged on for several years. He brought charges of sexual misconduct against Leadbeater, although the boys completely denied there was any truth in these allegations. The case went through several courts in England and was finally thrown out by the Privy Council, but by this time the father had become completely estranged from his sons. Later on, when Krishna and Nitya returned to India after an absence of ten years, they made a special point of going to see their father, in the hope of being reconciled with him. According to Krishna's biographer, Mary Lutyens, when Krishna and Nitya paid their visit, they prostrated themselves and touched their father's feet with their foreheads, as is the custom in India. Their father immediately went and washed his feet, declaring them defiled by the touch of pariahs.

Between 1909 and 1929, during the most formative years of his life, from age fourteen to thirty-four, Krishnamurti was almost constantly under the influence of the Theosophical Society. Soon after Leadbeater discovered him, the Theosophists formed a special group called the Order of the Star in the East (later the Order of the Star) to facilitate the mission they foresaw for him. The group, composed of the most senior members of the inner circle of Theosophy and many others, was designed to prepare people to receive the new Messiah or World Teacher who was to inhabit Krishna's body and speak through him. They launched a journal called *The Herald of the Star,* later *The Star Review,* with Krishnamurti as its nominal editor. It contained accounts of many past lives of the reincarnating ego of Krishnamurti under the "star name" of Alcyone. In these accounts many of the leaders of the Theosophical Society, under their star names, played significant roles.

Krishnamurti and his younger brother spent most of this period in England, France and the United States, with only a few visits to

India to attend Theosophical Society conventions. Wherever they went they were always in the company of other Theosophists, a situation which both of them sometimes found stifling, owing to the pious and holy atmosphere associated with the Theosophical circles. As they entered mature adulthood in this milieu that allowed them no independence of time, money or accommodation, and left no room for youthful exuberance, the brothers began to find Theosophy and its demands quite tiresome. Nitya, with a nature more robust than Krishna's, began to develop a loathing for the whole thing and longed to escape from it, but they were completely beholden to the Theosophical Society and its president, Mrs. Besant, not only for the care, protection and livelihood they needed, but also for the acceptance and honor they were accorded in Theosophical circles.

There were compensations, of course, for this captivity. Krishna and Nitya were the most valued and prized persons in the esoteric circles of Theosophy. At a time when a great many English people treated Indians worse than their dogs, regarding them as members of a subhuman race, quite a few members of the Theosophical Society, particularly the ladies of the English nobility, risked a great deal for the favor of a look, a touch or a letter from the coming Messiah or his brother. They longed to serve them with their mind, body and soul, regardless of their husbands' disapproval of this rechanneling of time, money and affection away from their own families. Lady Emily Lutyens can serve as an example. She was a daughter of the first Earl of Lytton, who had been a Viceroy of India. From their first meeting in 1911 until her death in 1964, Lady Emily and Krishnamurti had the warmest of relationships—often arousing suspicion and jealousy, though in Krishnamurti's eyes, she was like his dear mother.

However trapped Krishna and Nitya felt, their cages were certainly handsomely gilded. The following account of their accommodations in 1919, a year of great political and social turmoil in India, gives a fairly typical picture of the style in which they lived during their stay in the West:

> *Krishna and Nitya spent the summer partly at Old Lodge, Ashdown Forest, where they had stayed in 1912, and partly at West Side House, Wimbledon, which Miss Dodge shared with Lady De La Warr. In this large house with its beautiful garden, including*

*two tennis courts, the boys were surrounded
with every imaginable luxury, for Miss
Dodge lived in great style.*

*In July the boys went to stay with Lady
De La Warr at a house she had taken by
the sea in Scotland, at Gullane in East
Lothian on the outskirts of the famous
championship golf course at Muirfield;
playing golf every day, Krishna became a
scratch player. According to Mrs. Jean
Bindley, National Representative of the Order of the Star in the East for Scotland,
Krishna won a championship at Gullane
which, he told her, was the proudest moment of his life.*

*They wore pale gray spats, had their
shoes made at Lobb's (their feet were far
too narrow for ready-made shoes), their
suits at Myers and Mortimer, their shirts at
Beale and Inman, bought their ties at
Liberty's, and had their hair cut at
Trumper's . . . .[3]*

It could not have been easy to lay aside
these golden chains. Such experiences had a
very strong influence on the two brothers and
shaped Krishnamurti's attitude towards the re-

petitive, dull and uncreative jobs ordinary people have to engage in to make ends meet.

Even their many upper class connections, however, could not get the boys into Cambridge or Oxford. Neither university was willing to accept the Indian boy who had been proclaimed the coming Messiah, nor was either willing to accept his brother, when both boys had been accused of homosexuality by their own father. Krishna and Nitya then took the entrance examination for the University of London. Nitya succeeded and went on to study for the bar, but Krishna never managed to pass the examination, even after repeated attempts. He was finally advised to abandon that course. This outcome could hardly fail to deepen his dependence on the Theosophical circles and also his wish for independence from them.

Nitya even went so far as to dabble in some money-making schemes; he longed so much to be his own man. Krishna was by nature more in harmony than Nitya with the ideal image of a pure and high spirit that the Theosophical Society projected on him and was not at all drawn to base pursuits and pleasures. It is interesting to note, however, that when, in 1926, a film company offered Krishna $5,000 a week to play the title role in scenes from the life of the Buddha, the offer gave him "the satisfactory feeling that he could always earn his own living if the need arose." [4] This feeling that he could make his own way financially must have helped him come to the decision to break away from the Theosophical Society a few years later. Before that period he seems to have vacillated for several years between a wish to free himself from the Theosophists and a wish to live up to their expectations. Periodically, he exhorted himself to be more serious, or to work harder at meditation, or to develop a sound philosophy of life.

It is difficult to determine the exact nature of the training that Krishnamurti received in the Theosophical circles. Most of what he learned seems to have been a result of the atmosphere of holiness around the Theosophical Society. He was supposed to associate with the right people and to think lofty thoughts, to stay clear of the various sins and forbidden pleasures of sexuality, alcohol and meat, and to be constantly receptive to the messages—received while in the astral body rather than in the physical—from Lord Maitreya or from the Masters and other members of the occult hier-

archy. These influences left a lasting mark on
Krishnamurti even after he had completely broken away from Theosophy and the associated
occult hierarchy of Masters and Apostles. It is
ironic, for example, that Krishnamurti, who
among contemporary spiritual teachers was
perhaps the most self-consciously antitradi-
tional, should have been so thoroughly a traditional Hindu in his other-worldly attitude towards food, money and sex.

While he was associated with the Theosophists, Krishna was exposed to the scrip-
tures of many of the religions of the world.
Among the Eastern ones, he seems to have been
particularly struck by the life and teachings of
the Buddha. In the early twenties, for example,
he read aloud to his Theosophical associates
from *The Buddha's Way of Virtue*. At least one
passage sufficiently impressed him that he cop-
ied it out for Lady Emily: "All conquering and
all knowing am I, detached, untainted, untram-
meled, wholly freed by destruction of desire.
Whom shall I call Teacher? Myself found the
way." [5] The style of the book also seems to
have found its way into some of Krishnamurti's
own later utterances.

Among the various books of the Bible, his favorite was *The Song of Songs,* as he told me himself. [6] Krishnamurti was a poet and a lover at heart, especially receptive to nature's beauty and to spiritual truth. Somewhat in the fashion of St. John of the Cross, the great Spanish mystic of the sixteenth century, he experienced the soul as feminine in relation to God, her Beloved, and spoke of the Beloved with feminine sensitivity:

> *I have been united with my Beloved, and my Beloved and I will wander together the face of the earth . . . It is no good asking me who is the Beloved. Of what use is explanation? For you will not understand the Beloved until you are able to see Him in every animal, in every blade of grass, in every person that is suffering, in every individual.* [7]

Although later in life Krishnamurti often claimed never to have read the Gospels, this is highly unlikely, given the general religious orientation of the Theosophists who brought him up and the constant parallels drawn—especially by Annie Besant—between his life and that of Jesus Christ. He either completely forgot that he had read the Gospels, as he seems to have forgotten many other important details of his life prior to the powerful transformational processes he underwent in the second half of the 1920s, or he had a very strong residual reaction against them, perhaps owing to the comparisons made earlier between his own life and that of Jesus.

The latter possibility can by no means be eliminated. One often had the impression of such reactions in Krishnamurti, with the accompanying violence, as if in his old age he was still fighting the battles of his youth, trying to free himself from the shrinking walls of the prison he had felt himself to be in. It is particularly noteworthy that in his conversations and talks he frequently—and often without any relevance to the topic at hand—returned to harangues against the Brahmins and the Christians, the only two religious groups with whom he had any prolonged contact during his Theosophical phase. It was quite difficult indeed to discover any compassion, charity or love in him when he happened to mention either of these two groups. A similar and very deep reaction, with the same sort of emotional vehemence, existed in him against teachers, gurus, hierarchies and spiritual paths—in fact, against any sort of discipline or process. It was as if he had two distinct parts. His deep spiritual essence could soar without effort like an angel in the clear skies of Truth. When he spoke from that part, it was as if the heavenly choir were singing. The listener felt blessed and in total accord. Then there was the relatively superficial personality, formed by his personal history and his struggles to be free of spiritual tyranny. This part was born of conditioning and not of insight. When it took over, it was like the discordant note introduced by the uninvited thirteenth fairy in the tale of *Sleeping Beauty.* [8]

The two important personal influences in Krishnamurti's life were his mother and his younger brother, Nitya. After his mother died, for the rest of his life, he sought and found women who would mother him, take care of his ordinary needs and give him protective affection. More than to any other aspect of the eternal feminine—lover, daughter, sister—he was drawn to that of mother. During the various painful spiritual processes that he underwent, which caused him immense physical and psychological suffering, he always wanted women—especially youthful and pure virgins—to be near him and look after him. Often, when he was in pain or in trance, he would refer to them as mother. As he himself often said, the religious mind is an innocent mind, and the mark of innocence is its vulnerability. All who were close to Krishnamurti and cared for him recognized this vulnerability and tried to protect him. For the women around him, the only permissible public role seems to have been that of mother.

In his private life, matters seem to have been quite different. Several years after Krishnamurti's death, Radha Rajagopal Sloss published details of a long-lasting affair in the 1930s and 1940s between Krishnamurti and Rosalind Rajagopal, her mother.[9] These revelations of the enormous gulf between the public stance and the private life of Krishnamurti have caused many of Krishnamurti's admirers and devotees considerable discomfort. Not unexpectedly, there have been shocks of recognition, denials of the scandal, and attempts to whitewash Krishnamurti as well as to vilify Ms. Sloss. The ethical problem posed by the behavior of Krishnamurti cannot be ignored. Anyone who lives in the society and makes moral proclamations about it is obliged to be forthright and consistent in word and deed. However, some understanding of the inconsistency between the public stance of Krishnamurti and his private actions might emerge with a recognition of the radical transformation which had taken place in Krishnamurti. About his inner spiritual being it is possible to say, with Plotinus, that "this man has now become another and is neither himself nor his own" (*Enneads* iv. 9.10).

This radical split in Krishnamurti, which has already been remarked upon earlier in this article in a different context, may be a form of the "sacred schizophrenia," not unknown in mystical literature. There was Krishnamurti, the vessel of great revelation from on high, but also Krishnamurti the man subject to his personal conditioning, desires and needs. These two parts were distinct and of entirely different orders of importance and significance. From the higher part, the lower, more personal aspects may not be given much importance. They may not even be recognized or remembered or identified as belonging to the self. There are phases in mystical life in which a sharp discontinuity is emphasized between the spirit and the body-mind, or between "heaven" and "earth." It can be said that the ability to separate the inner or higher Self from the lower self is a mark of spiritual development. But the ability to bring the two parts together intentionally and with freedom is a sign of divine wisdom and incarnation.

There is a story in one of the *Puranas* about the God incarnate Krishna, who lived a long time ago, as he lives now, with his consort Radha. The two lived by a riverbank as householders. One day they received a message from Durvasa, a sage well-known for his spiritual austerities and for his short temper. He was on the other side of the river with a thousand of his followers and wished to be fed. As proper householders, Krishna and Radha undertook to do their part in the maintenance of *dharma* (order) by preparing food for the mendicants. When Radha was ready to carry the food across to the other shore, she saw the river in full spate and wondered how she could get across. Krishna said, "Go to the river and say 'If Krishna is eternally celibate, O River, subside!'" Radha knew well the power of uttering the true word, but was this a word of truth? Of all people, she ought to know about the amorous delights of Krishna! She smiled to herself, went to the river and asked her to subside if Krishna was eternally celibate. Somewhat to her surprise, the river subsided. She went across and took the food to the sage Durvasa, who was well pleased and ate heartily along with his disciples. When it was time for Radha to return, she again saw the river in full spate and asked the sage for help. The sage said, "Go to the river and say, 'If Durvasa is eternally fasting, O River, subside!'" Radha had just seen the sage eat. She smiled to herself, went to the river and asked her to subside if Durvasa was eternally fasting. The river subsided, and Radha returned home to Krishna, there to continue the delightful play of *Prakriti*.

It was then she realized the truth of what Krishna taught Arjuna,

> *All action is verily done by* Prakriti *[Nature] and the Self is not the doer . . . He who is above the* gunas *[constituents of Prakriti] does not abhor illumination nor impulsion to action nor delusion when they occur, nor longs for them when they cease (Bhagavad Gita* 13:29, 14:22*).*

The delicate and subtle relationship between Purusha and Prakriti, between consciousness and nature, has been of perennial interest to the sages and spiritual masters. A sage says in the *Rig Veda*,

*Two birds, inseparable companions, are
perched on the same tree; one eats the sweet
fruit and the other looks on without eating
(I.164.20).*

This insight was considered of great significance
and was repeated in precisely the same words
in *Mundaka Upanishad* (III.I.1) and in
Shvetashvatara Upanishad (IV.6). It is worth
emphasizing that these two birds are inseparable. In the same way, a human being is not
complete and whole without the aspect of
Prakriti, which experiences the domain of space
and time and acts in the world, or without the
Purusha aspect, which watches but remains
transcendent. An especially striking image is
used by Ishvarakrishna, the compiler of the
ancient text of *Samkhyakarika,* who pointed
out that "Purusha without Prakriti is lame, and
Prakriti without Purusha is blind."

In the case of Krishnamurti the difficulty is not in the fact that he cherished feminine companionship and love. That is quite
natural, which is to say that his action was per-
fectly consonant with enjoying the play of
Prakriti. The problem more lay in the limited
view of human wholeness which led him and
his followers to a denial of what is and of parts

of themselves rather than to a celebration of and a freedom from Prakriti.

Krishnamurti's relationships with men were different from his relationships with women. Men who were close to him could try to place themselves in the role of his younger brother Nitya, and an occasional person succeeded for a while. By all accounts, these two brothers had been very close to each other. They were discovered together, they traveled together and lived together most of the time until Nitya's death in 1925. Krishnamurti himself described his relationship with his brother:

> *Silence was a special delight to both of us, as then it was so easy to understand each other's thoughts and feelings. Occasional irritation with each other was by no means forgotten but it never went very far as it passed off in a few minutes, we used to sing comic songs or chant together as the occasion demanded. We both often liked the same cloud, the same tree and the same music. We had great fun in life, though we were of different temperaments. We somehow understood each other without effort.* [10]

In accordance with the explicit instructions of the Masters in the occult world, the Theosophists had regarded Nitya as absolutely essential to the mission for which Krishnamurti was being prepared. In November, 1925, Nitya was very sick in Ojai, California. It was one of the very few occasions when Krishna traveled without him. He had an unquestioning faith that the Masters would prolong Nitya's life, since his brother was necessary to his own life-mission. During the sea voyage—on his way to India to attend a Theosophical Society congress—he received the news of Nitya's death. According to the person who was sharing the cabin with Krishna on this voyage, the news

broke him completely; it did more—his entire philosophy of life—the implicit faith in the future as outlined by Mrs. Besant and Mr. Leadbeater, Nitya's vital part in it, all appeared shattered at that moment . . . At night he would sob and moan and cry out for Nitya, sometimes in his native Telugu which in his waking consciousness he could not speak. Day after day we watched him, heart-broken, disillusioned. Day after day he seemed to change, gripping himself together in an effort to face life—but without

Nitya. He was going through an inner revolution, finding new strength.[11]

By the time the voyage ended, Krishnamurti had found a different inner stand. He had been strengthened by the suffering caused by his brother's death:

An old dream is dead and a new one is being born, as a flower that pushes through the solid earth. A new vision is coming into being and a new consciousness is being unfolded . . . A new thrill and a new throb of the same life is being felt. A new strength born of suffering is pulsating in the veins and a new sympathy and understanding is being born out of the past suffering. A greater desire to see others suffer less and if they must suffer to see that they bear it nobly and come out of it without too many scars. I have wept but I do not want others to weep but if they do I now know what it means . . . I have seen my brother . . . On the physical plane we could be separated and now we are inseparable . . . For my brother and I are one. As Krishnamurti I now have greater zeal, greater faith, greater sympathy and greater love for there is also in me the body, the

Being, of Nityananda . . . I know how to weep still, but that is human. I know now, with greater certainty than ever before, that there is real beauty in life, real happiness that cannot be shattered by any physical happening, a great strength which cannot be weakened by passing events, and a great love which is permanent, imperishable and unconquerable. [12]

In August 1922, Krishnamurti underwent a series of experiences which radically changed his life and the lives of those who were near him at that time. His own description of these experiences is most illuminating with respect to the processes involved and their authenticity. [13] A particularly significant experience commenced on the seventeenth of August. Here is an excerpt of a report given by Krishnamurti himself, written down within two days of the events described:

. . . Since August 3rd, I meditated regularly for about thirty minutes every morning. I could, to my astonishment, concentrate with considerable ease, and within a few days I began to see clearly where I had failed and where I was failing. Immediately I set about, consciously, to annihilate the wrong

accumulations of the past years. With the same deliberation I set about to find out ways and means to achieve my aim. First I realized that I had to harmonize all my other bodies with the Buddhic plane [a high plane of consciousness] and to bring about this happy combination I had to find out what my ego wanted on the Buddhic plane. To harmonize the various bodies I had to keep them vibrating at the same rate as the Buddhic, and to do this I had to find out what was the vital interest of the Buddhic. With ease which rather astonished me I found the main interest on the high plane was to serve the Lord Maitreya and the Masters. With that idea clear in my mind I had to direct and control the other bodies to act and to think the same as on the noble and spiritual plane. During that period of less than three weeks, I concentrated to keep in mind the image of Lord Maitreya throughout the entire day, and I found no difficulty in doing this. I found that I was getting calmer and more serene. My whole outlook on life was changed.

Then on the 17th August, I felt acute pain at the nape of my neck and I had to cut down my meditation to fifteen minutes.

The pain instead of getting better as I had hoped grew worse. The climax was reached on the 19th. I could not think, nor was I able to do anything, and I was forced by friends here to retire to bed. Then I became almost unconscious, though I was well aware of what was happening around me. I came to myself at about noon each day. On the first day while I was in that state and more conscious of the things around me, I had the first most extraordinary experience. There was a man mending the road; that man was myself; the pickaxe he held was myself; the very stone which he was breaking up was a part of me; the tender blade of grass was my very being, and the tree beside the man was myself . . . I was in everything, or rather everything was in me, inanimate and animate, the mountain, the worm, and all breathing things. . .

The morning of the next day . . . My head was pretty bad and the top part felt as though many needles were being driven in . . . When I had sat thus [cross-legged in the meditation posture] for some time, I felt myself going out of my body, I saw myself sitting down with the delicate tender leaves of the tree over me. I was facing the east.

*In front of me was my body and over my
head I saw the Star, bright and clear. Then
I could feel the vibrations of the Lord Buddha; I beheld Lord Maitreya and Master
K.H. [Koot Hoomi], I was so happy, calm
and at peace. I could still see my body and
I was hovering near it. There was such profound calmness both in the air and within
myself, the calmness of the bottom of a deep
unfathomable lake. Like the lake, I felt my
physical body, with its mind and emotions,
could be ruffled on the surface but nothing, nay nothing, could disturb the calmness of my soul. The Presence of the mighty
Beings was with me for some time and then
They were gone. I was supremely happy,
for I had seen. Nothing could ever be the
same. I have drunk at the clear and pure
waters at the source of the fountain of life
and my thirst was appeased. Never more
could I be thirsty, never more could I be in
utter darkness. I have seen the Light. I have
touched compassion which heals all sorrow
and suffering; it is not for myself, but for
the world. I have stood on the mountain
top and gazed at the mighty Beings . . . The
fountain of Truth has been revealed to me
and the darkness has been dispersed. Love*

in all its glory has intoxicated my heart;
my heart can never be closed. I have drunk
at the fountain of Joy and eternal Beauty.
I am God-intoxicated. [14]

Krishnamurti's experience was so powerful that even his biographer, writing more
than fifty years later, decided that after this point
in his life story she would refer to him simply
as *K*, precisely as he did himself, referring to
himself in the third person. (While addressing
him, his friends and followers called him
Krishnaji, the respectful suffix *ji* being added
in the traditional Indian manner.) From that
time in August, 1922, when the explicit process of what can only be called the *alchemical*
transformation of K's planetary body (including the emotions and the mind) began, he had
many periods of intense physical pain and suffering as his body was reconstituted, cell by
cell, as it seems, by forces immeasurably higher
than himself. He himself referred to this as
"the process," and he experienced it off and
on even into old age in a mild form, as is clear
from the many entries in his *Notebook* written
in 1961–62.

Here is his own description of it, given in 1922:

> *. . . All the time, I have a violent pain in my head & the nape of my neck & can't bear the touch of anyone. Also during that time, I become very sensitive, can't bear a sound, however small it may be . . . .* [15]

His brother concluded at that time that what K was experiencing was an awakening of *kundalini*—which, according to the occultists, is coiled-up cosmic energy at the base of the spine that can, by proper practices and right living, be aroused and bring about a spiritual transformation of the human being. About two years later, this process came to a climax, which he described to Lady Emily:

> *. . . Last 10 days, it has been really strenuous, my spine & neck have been going very strong and day before yesterday, the 27th [February, 1922] I had an extraordinary evening. Whatever it is, the force or whatever one calls the bally thing, came up my spine, up to the nape of my neck, then it separated into two, one going to the right & the other to the left of my head till they met between the two eyes, just above my nose.*

There was a kind of flame and I saw the Lord & the Master. It was a tremendous night. Of course, the whole thing was painful, in the extreme. [16]

It is clear that K himself never doubted that all this pain was necessary and that all his experiences were genuine. It does not seem to have even occurred to him to consult a doctor or to take pain-relieving drugs. Some people who had known him for a very long time had no doubt that he was *the Sacrifice* who must relinquish any concern for himself or for his pleasure or pain, and that he had to respond to what was demanded of him, like a suffering servant.

As his experience deepened, and as he became more and more aware of the egotistic purposes to which the various stages of "initiation" and the various official positions within the Theosophical circles could be put, he became more and more disenchanted with the entire Theosophical structure and gradually with all forms which allow fear and temptation to corrupt the human heart. It was his very great respect for Annie Besant and his sense of gratitude that made him hesitate to debunk the Masters, the occult hierarchy and the superstructure of the Theosophical Society publicly, but his skepticism became more and more evident to the people close to him, causing more and more pain to the leaders of the Society. Already in 1928, at one of the meetings in Holland, he had warned people against becoming his disciples:

> I say again that I have no disciples. Everyone of you is a disciple of the Truth if you understand the Truth and do not follow individuals . . . The only manner of attaining Truth [is] to become disciples of the Truth itself without a mediator . . . Truth does not give hope; it gives understanding . . . I refuse to be your crutch. I am not going to be brought into a cage for your worship . . . I am not concerned with societies, with religions, with dogmas, but I am concerned with life because I am Life. [17]

He could not for very long continue with the sort of double life he had been leading for the previous five years—progressively disillusioned with all forms, and in particular with those of the Theosophical Society—but he did not want to hurt anyone, especially not Mrs. Besant, whom he always revered as his mother. Finally, on August 2, 1929, he dissolved the Order of the Star with the memorable speech in which he declared that "Truth is a pathless land," a part of which was quoted at the beginning of this essay.

Krishnamurti's words and actions shook the Theosophical Society to its core and caused a great split from which it has not yet recovered. Many people, including Mrs. Besant, remained faithful to K however hard they found it to understand and to accept him. But Leadbeater declared that "the Coming has gone wrong," and went his own way. After the death of Mrs. Besant in September, 1933, K's connection with the Theosophical Society was completely broken until nearly fifty years later, when, in January, 1983, on the invitation of Radha Burnier, the president of the Society, K planted a tree in the compound of the Society headquarters in Adyar. To many serious people in the Theosophical movement, Krishnamurti seems to be a Theosophist, a slightly aberrant one, to be sure, but still recognizably Theosophical, with a teaching very much along the lines of the *Voice of the Silence*.

Krishnamurti's years of physical agony culminated in 1932 at Ojai, California. When he reached a new level of consciousness, he seems to have almost entirely lost memory of his life before that period. It was almost like a new birth physically for him. Now this Brahmin boy was a *dvija*, a twice-born, not only in hope and tradition, but in fact. Having entered the Immensity (in Sanskrit, *Brahman*)—"I am that full flame which is the glory of life," as he said—he was neither a Brahmin nor anyone else in particular. For nearly the last sixty years of his life, he traveled all over the globe, constantly trying to express, with enormous passion and suffering, the same inexpressible Truth again and again in different words. He suffered at the incomprehension of his hearers, but went on teaching. As he himself said, a flower does not decide whether or not to give out perfume: it is in its very nature to do so. That is what makes it a flower. Just as a flower gives out fragrance, Krishnamurti taught. He could not help it.

He kept traveling and teaching, under an inner compulsion, until his death in February, 1986. It was as if he were directed by some higher force and had no personal choice. Just ten days before his death, at the age of nearly ninety-one, he had a tape recording made of something he wanted to say.

I was telling them this morning—for seventy years that super-energy—no—that immense energy, immense intelligence, has been using this body. I don't think people realize what tremendous energy and intelligence went through this body—there's twelve-cylinder engine. And for seventy years—was a pretty long time—and now the body can't stand any more. Nobody, unless the body has been prepared, very carefully, protected and so on—nobody can understand what went through this body. Nobody. Don't anybody pretend. Nobody. I repeat this: nobody amongst us or the public, know what went on. I know they don't. And now after seventy years it has come to an end. Not that intelligence and energy—it's somewhat here, every day, and especially at night. And after seventy years the body can't stand it—can't stand any more. It can't. The Indians have a lot of damned superstitions about this—that you will and the body goes—and all that kind of nonsense. You won't find another body like this, or that supreme intelligence, operating in a body for many hundred years. You won't see it again. When he goes, it goes. There is no consciousness left behind of that consciousness, of that state. They'll all pretend or try to imagine they can get into touch with that. Perhaps they will somewhat if they live the teachings. But nobody has done it. Nobody. And so that's that. [18]

❖   ❖   ❖   ❖

What is K's teaching? It is a teaching which demands a mutation of the human being into another dimension, a dimension of being which is not of thought. This spiritual dimension is not created by the mind, nor is it an acquisition or an achievement of any sort. This dimension is manifested precisely when there is no center of ambition in the self that wants possessions or struggles for achievement. It is the dimension of insight, a special sort of intelligence that can express itself through thought, but has its origin beyond thought and is not conditioned by thought nor brought about by it. Thought operates in time—in the past or in the future, in memory or in anticipation. Within the dimension of time, thought can be good, orderly, coherent and logical, or it can be incoherent and irrational. Rational and coherent thought can lead to knowledge that can be useful, as scientific and technological knowledge are useful. But however orderly this thought is, however vast the knowledge, it cannot offer the insight requisite for solving fundamental human problems. Only in the awakening of the intelligence which is beyond thought and beyond time can the knots of ignorance, compulsion and repetition be dissolved.

It is extremely difficult to say anything about insight, which exists in its fullness only as it comes into being. How can what is in flight be fixed in a picture, a poem or some other description, unless the articulation made in a moment of insight triggers an internal re-ordering that permits a similarly intense and clear insight in the listener or the reader? The moment it is given expression in speaking or in writing, it operates in the domain of thought, time and knowledge. An insight which has been expressed is something that one knows of and thinks about, to which one reacts or around which one reasons. True action takes place only in the moment of the awakening of insight. Otherwise action is in fact a reaction to the *memory* of insight, whether it is one's own insight or someone else's.

The moment of insight is *in* time but it is not *of* time. It is a timeless moment, a point of intersection of eternity and time. Eternity is not merely an extension of time without end. It is a dimension of being altogether different from time. As Krishnamurti said, "The eternal is not everlasting." The insight that arises from beyond thought carries with it a freshness and an innocence which are the chief characteristics of the religious mind. Listening to Krishnamurti from an external perspective, examining and analyzing his teaching, one might say that he had been saying the same thing for decades. It may even be true, as far as the words and the formulations are concerned: one had heard them before. But for Krishnamurti, speaking and teaching were acts of love. The accompanying words and actions may have been the same time after time, but each time there was a freshness of insight, an abundance of passion and an urgency of expression. His timeless insight poured out of him with love and compassion for those around him.

As he became exhausted with this out-pouring, sometimes a great sadness came over him. Once, not long before his death, he said to me, with his eyes full of sorrow, "No one understands what I have been saying for the last sixty years. No one." This was not directed at anyone in particular, not even at me, though no doubt I too had added to K's sorrow by not understanding.

Soon his cup was filled again, and he was ready to speak to anyone who would listen. He neither spoke because he liked to, nor was he able to stop because he would like to: he did what he had to do. In the choiceless awareness that he had, he saw that there was only one thing that he had to do, and he did it.

Freedom exists in that choiceless awareness and in the accompanying action: freedom from fear, from memory and anticipation, from time and all the things of time. This freedom is a freedom from the known, for it is the known which is the source of fear, not the unknown. What is truly unknown, and allowed to be unknown, cannot cause fear. It is the imagined continuation or termination of what is known that produces fear. It is the clinging to what one knows and to the center from

which one knows that keeps one bound by
time and by the ego. If one sees that these
keep one in bondage and sorrow, then the need
for a complete reorientation and a total revolution asserts itself. What is needed is a radical
break from all that leads to bondage and suffering. What is required is freedom from the
tyranny of one's own ego—from the tyranny
of all that one has been taught and the tyranny
of one's own inclinations and one's own style.
What is necessary is freedom from authority—
from external authority, of course, but also from
the internal authority of oneself. Otherwise,
future moments are always conditioned by what
one knew or experienced in the past. Freedom from the grooves created by one's own
past knowledge and experience is what can
permit one to be fresh in the new moment and
not always to react through prejudice and conditioning.

For Krishnamurti thought leads to fragmentation, and subsequently to fear and sorrow, just as for the Buddha *tanha* (selfish craving) leads to *dukkha* (sorrow), or for the
Vedantist ignorance leads to illusion. In all of
these teachings, total attention in the state of
meditation is required to dissolve sorrow, fear
and illusion in the clear light of Intelligence

and Truth. The meditative mind, open, whole and quiet, is the religious mind. This religious mind is natural, and ultimately this state of mind is reached by effortless being—just as an oak tree is the natural unfolding of an acorn. Patanjali's *Yoga Sutra*, in the final chapter on Enlightenment, puts it quite simply: "Any transformation into a new state of being is the result of fullness of Nature unfolding inherent potential" (4:2).

The difficulty comes with the need for the training of this total attention. It is for this that the Eightfold Path of the Buddha and the practices recommended in the earlier chapters of the *Yoga Sutra* exist.   Krishnamurti himself provided an excellent example of right living, right thinking, right posture and other preliminary and necessary practices. He no doubt conveyed some of this to his followers. But he had a strange insistence about the futility and harmfulness of practices, disciplines and teachings, and certainly of teachers and gurus. In his presence it was easy to forget that although consummate musicians do play without effort, as if the music played itself through them, this ease is the fruit of long and hard struggle with scales and exercises.

In a conversation in Madras in January, 1983, Krishnamurti said to me that the Intelligence beyond thought is just there, like the air, and that it does not need to be created by discipline or effort. "All one needs to do is to open the window," he said. But if one sees the windows are painted shut and need a lot of scraping before they can be opened, how does one scrape? When asked about the difficulty of sustaining attention, K replied that it is only inattention that fluctuates. That is true; but it still disturbs the mind. If weeds are choking a garden, no amount of water and sunshine would suffice to produce beautiful flowers. To quote the *Yoga Sutra* again,

> *The apparent causes of a transformation do not in fact bring it about. They merely remove the obstacles to natural growth, as a farmer clears the ground for his crops (4:3).*

As time went on, even though there was a change in the phrases and words that K used, he always tried to bring us back to look at ourselves radically and totally. That look, that passionate insight, alone can bring about the transformation. Towards the end of his life, he did occasionally refer to his insights

and ideas as "this teaching," and to himself as
a "teacher." In a talk to some teachers in India
he said, "I am your teacher, not your guru." [19]
This was quite a shift for him, although in his
continued reaction against authority he forgot
that *guru* is just a Sanskrit word for teacher. In
any case, it can be said with certainty that anyone who met Krishnamurti with an open mind
came away convinced that he or she had been
in the presence of a very great man, a beacon
of light. One could not help loving him and
recognizing in him a free man. He was a distant and a profound musician of the spirit to
whom we need to listen:

> *Silence has many qualities . . . There is
> the silence between two noises, the silence
> between two notes, the widening silence be-
> tween two thoughts. There is that peculiar
> quiet pervading silence that comes on an
> evening in the country, there is the silence
> through which you hear the bark of a dog
> in the distance or the whistle of a train as it
> comes up a steep grade; the silence of a
> house when everybody has gone to sleep,
> and the peculiar emphasis when you wake
> up in the middle of the night and listen to
> an owl hooting in the valley . . . there is the
> silence of the mind which is never touched*

by any noise, any thought or by the passing wind of experience. It is the silence which is innocent, and so endless. When there is silence of the mind, action springs from it, and this action does not cause confusion or misery . . . The meditative mind flows in this silence, and love is the way of this mind. In this silence there is bliss and laughter.

NOTES

[1] Quoted in Mary Lutyens, *Krishnamurti: The Years of Awakening* (New York: Farrar, Straus, Giroux, 1975) pp. 272-275.

[2] According to the Theosophists, Lord Maitreya, a World Teacher, had twice taken possession of a human body in order to bring a new teaching during a world crisis: first as Sri Krishna in the fourth century B.C.E. and then as Jesus Christ. They expected that he would come again in a human form to give a new teaching to the world. It should be noted that Maitreya is not the Buddha, who is a still higher spiritual entity in the Theosophical hierarchy. He is, however, a Bodhisattva, which is to say, a future Buddha.

[3] Lutyens, *Krishnamurti: Awakening,* pp. 104-107.

[4] Ibid., p. 237.

[5] Ibid., p. 120.

[6] See Ravi Ravindra,"The Mill and the Mill-Pond: A Twenty-year Conversation with J. Krishnamurti," *The American Theosophist,* vol. 74, 1986, pp. 298-303. (Reproduced in this volume.)

[7] Quoted in Lutyens, *Krishnamurti: Awakening,* p. 250.

[8] I was told in 1982 by Dora Kunz, who was at that time the president of the Theosophical Society in America, and who had known Krishnamurti since 1922 and had herself been a student of Leadbeater for a few years, that Krishnamurti felt chagrined with, and betrayed by, Leadbeater, who, it appeared to Krishnamurti, was refusing to see him while spending time with other, less important, people. Krishnamurti seems to have been too occupied with his own deep searchings and the illness of his brother Nitya to realize that Leadbeater was very sick himself, had had several heart attacks and needed to save his energy by not exposing himself to Krishnamurti's rather violent rejection of anything told to him at that time. It is quite possible that the disappointment caused in Krishnamurti by his father's "betrayal" of him and later by what he perceived as this surrogate father's rejection of him is the psychological cause of his deep reaction, not only against Brahmins and Christians, but also against all authority figures—teachers, gurus, Masters and God.

[9] See Radha Rajagopal Sloss, *Lives in the Shadow with J. Krishnamurti* (London: Bloomsbury, 1991).

[10] Quoted in Lutyens, *Krishnamurti: Awakening,* p. 220.

[11] Lutyens, Krishnamurti: *Awakening,* p. 220. It appears that with the death of Nitya, that part of Krishnamurti which could be involved in *personal* relationship with anyone also died.

[12] Lutyens, *Krishnamurti: Awakening,* pp. 220-221.

[13] Full details of these experiences are given in Lutyens, *Krishnamurti: Awakening,* pp. 152-188. The brief excerpts quoted here are taken from that book. The material in the square brackets has been slightly emended.

[14] Lutyens, *Krishnamurti: Awakening,* pp. 158-160.

[15] Ibid., p. 165.

[16] Ibid., p. 186.

[17] Ibid., pp. 261-262.

[18] Quoted in Mary Lutyens, *The Life and Death of Krishnamurti* (London: John Murray Publishers, 1990), p. 206.

[19] Pupul Jayakar and Sunanda Patwardhan (editors), *Within the Mind: On J. Krishnamurti* (Madras, India: Krishnamurti Foundation India, 1982), p. 148.

It is only in silence that love can exist. The quality of love is not born out of desire, conflict and all the rest of the ugliness and torture: it comes into being with the understanding of time, space, desire, pleasure; it is then that it is seen that love is not desire and pleasure. That innocent mind can solve all the problems and all the challenges that it meets. It is completely aware of all the problems of man— and it becomes immeasureable. To such a mind, there is no time and no death; to come upon such a mind one has to end sorrow; the ending of sorrow is the beginning of wisdom.

J. Krishnamurti

Now to find out if there is such a thing as the eternal, one has to understand what is time. Time is a most extraordinary thing—and I am not talking about chronological time, time by the watch, which is both obvious and necessary. I am talking about time as psychological continuity . . . And is it possible to live in this world without giving continuity to action, so that one comes to every action afresh? That is, can I die to each action throughout the day, so that the mind never accumulates and is therefore never contaminated by the past, but is always new, fresh, innocent? I say that such a thing is possible, that one can live in this way— but that does not mean it is real for you. You have to find out for yourself.

J. Krishnamurti

THE MILL AND THE MILL-POND:
A TWENTY-YEAR CONVERSATION
WITH J. KRISHNAMURTI

It was the fall of 1965 in New Delhi. My wife had asked me to deliver something to Mrs. Kitty Shivarao who had been very kind to her when she, four years earlier, had come to India as a volunteer from Canada. I went on my bicycle and came to a sudden stop in front of a very tall man sitting completely alone, on a wicker chair on the porch of the Shivarao house. I wondered if Mrs. Shivarao was in, and the man, who was extremely self-contained, said he would go in and look. Without any hurry, but without delay, he got up, went in, and returned to say that she was not in at that time, but I could wait until she came back. I do not recall why I could not wait; perhaps I had the usual haste of the young, especially of those recently returned from a long stay in the West. I handed over to him what I had to deliver to the lady of the house and rode away on my bicycle. But I kept looking back at this unusual man with an extraordinary presence sitting on the porch, until I fell off my bicycle, having crashed into a woman carrying a large bundle on her head.

Several months later, at Rajghat in Varanasi, where an interview with Krishnamurti had been arranged for me, I was in a great turmoil; I became more and more agitated as four o'clock, the appointed time of the meeting, approached. I was not sure what I needed to ask him. I knew that I needed a different kind of knowledge and education than I had obtained in the many schools and universities I had attended. I had become sadder and sadder the closer I had gotten to finishing my Ph.D.: the more I was certified as an educated person by the world, the clearer I was about my ignorance of myself. What little I had gathered about Krishnamurti, mostly from my wife who had taught for a year in one of his schools in India before we had met, and from the little that I had read by him, had convinced me that he offered the sort of influence I needed. Here, at last, I was going to meet the great man himself. What was I going to say to him? What did I need to know? What should I ask him?

Besides, how could he, or anybody else, say something that would really become a part of myself? After all, I had read what the Buddha had said, and I still behaved the way I did before. And what was I going to tell him about myself? What did I know of any value? What did I have of any value? What was my value? Why waste his time?

All these questions whirled around in my head, making me more and more restless as the time for my meeting with Krishnamurti approached. Then, suddenly, a great calm possessed me. I knew with certainty that I did not know, that nobody else could really tell me something deeply true unless I saw it myself directly, and that there was no escape from an encounter with myself, an encounter without fear and without self-importance. I had no idea what had brought about these realizations and the resulting calm; maybe it was the magic of this extraordinary man working even before I had met him. I walked over to his room with assurance and, precisely at the appointed hour, he opened his door. I was surprised to discover that the man in front of me was the same man I had met on the porch in New Delhi. I had difficulty accepting his actual physical size;

my first impression of him had no doubt been of his real spiritual height.

He asked me to sit down on the same divan on which he was sitting. Then, after a brief silence, he asked, "What can I do for you?" "Nothing," I said with clarity. "I have really nothing to ask you. I have come just to look at you." He smiled, and we sat in silence for a long time, just looking at each other. Then, no doubt having noticed my attention wandering, he asked what I did and what interested me. I told him, and I also told him about my dissatisfaction with what I had learned. My clarity was dwindling, and I was returning to my habitual and more discursive mode of thought. I asked him, "Is there life after death?" He said, "Why worry about death when you don't know anything about life?"

When it was time for me to leave, he took me to the window of his room perched over the River Ganga, overlooking the path which the Buddha had taken on his way to Sarnath after his enlightenment. That was the only time I understood why pilgrims over the centuries have regarded this river as sacred. There were dark, thick clouds over the majestic river, and a white bird was flying in and out

of the clouds, sometimes disappearing completely and at other times showing clearly its
innocent vulnerability. He put his hand on my
shoulder, and we stood there watching for a
little while; then he said, pointing to the bird
in the clouds over the river, "Life is like that:
sometimes you see it, sometimes you don't."
As I was leaving, he said simply, "We shall meet
again."

Many years ago I had written an article called "Letter to J. Krishnamurti" on the
invitation of the editors of *A Journal of Our
Time*. Rather than getting into an argument
with Krishnamurti in the article, for I rarely had
any doubt that he was right, I had attempted to
say where my own difficulties lay in trying to
follow what he had been saying for so many
years. This small article had ended with the
following:

> *I am troubled because I do not know how
> to reconcile the call I hear from your dis-
> tant shore with the realities where I am. It
> is clear that a bridge cannot be built from
> here to There. But can it be built from There
> to here?*

A couple of years after the article had
been published, there was an occasion for me

to spend some time with Krishnamurti at Ojai in California, the place where he felt most at home. We had a long and intense conversation in the evening, and we were going to meet again at breakfast the next morning. I had asked that he read my little article and respond when we met in the morning. I was eager to know what he would say. He said he liked the last sentence, and added, "A bridge can be built from There to here." He would not say much more about it, except to imply that that is what he had been talking about all these years.

Since I have been interested for a long time in the quality of attention and seeing which can bring about an action in oneself so that a radical change can take place naturally, from the inside, I asked Krishnamurti about it. For him thought leads to fragmentation and, subsequently, to fear and sorrow, as for the Buddha *tanha* (selfish craving) leads to *dukkha* (sorrow), or for the Vedantist *avidya* (ignorance) leads to *maya* (illusion). In all of these teachings, what is required for sorrow, fear and illusion to be dissolved in the clear light of intelligence and truth is total attention. I asked him about the nature of this attention, and said, "What I find in myself is the fluctuation of at-

tention." He said with emphasis, "What fluctuates is not attention. Only inattention fluctuates."

On another occasion he said to me,

*I am still very shy, but I used to be much
worse. I would stand behind the platform
from where I was supposed to speak to an
audience and shake. One day I saw the
total absurdity of it, and the shaking left
me. I was free of it for ever.*

In a conversation in Madras he said
that the intelligence beyond thought is just
there, like the air, and does not need to be
created by discipline or effort: "All one needs
to do is to open the window." I suggested that
most windows are painted shut and need a lot
of scraping before they can be opened, and
asked, "How does one scrape?" "Sir," he said
sadly, "You don't see that the house is on fire."

In his concern with the dangers of hierarchy, Krishnamurti frequently placed a great
deal of emphasis on being democratic. He
would often talk in a small group as if everyone were actually at the same level as himself
and had an equal right to express an opinion.
Soon, of course, he would get bored or impa-

tient with a mere exchange of opinions and speak with the force of clear seeing, commanding attention from everyone around him. On one of these occasions in India, he had given a long rope to many people's opinions about the nature of the religious mind. I had just flown in from North America and was not eager to spend the morning philosophizing or listening to various opinions. He was the one I wanted to hear; for I had understood some time ago that Krishnamurti had a completely unusual mind and that he saw many things with an extraordinary clarity not vouchsafed to many. On this occasion, anxious to hear him speak, I blurted out, "But, Krishna Ji, what do you have to say about it? After all, you are the cat with the meat." I realized immediately that I had not chosen a very felicitous American expression for the assembled company of vegetarians. After a brief pause, he smiled, relieving the tension created by my remark, and protested that he was not special. "Do you think K is a freak?" he said, referring to himself in the third person, using only the initial of his name, assuming it to be obvious that he wasn't. I was never convinced—nor was anyone else around him, as far as I could see—that he was not a freak.

So often, I had been completely frustrated by going around the same point with Krishnamurti. For example, his insistence that there can be a radical transformation instantaneously, without any discipline or path or guidance, and by my inability to even understand what he was saying, let alone do it. On one occasion, in a semi-public seminar, I said in despair, "There's no sense in carrying on. We keep going around the same mulberry bush. It's totally frustrating." "Sir, then why do you keep coming?" I knew that my coming had nothing to do with any reasons; so I said what was true, "Because I love you." One did not decide to love Krishnamurti any more than a flower decides to give fragrance, to use one of his favorite analogies.

Once when I was in London I learned that Krishnamurti was at Brockwood, not very far away. Naturally, I wanted to see him. Not succeeding in making a telephone connection with anybody there, I gave up after many attempts. Since on many occasions he had said, "You may come any time," I decided to drive over with a friend and take my chances. I wonder if the gods know how heavily guarded have to be the gates of paradise! One could say that there were lots of guardians at his gates;

and we had some difficulty, quite understand-
able to be sure, in getting close to the inner
sanctum. One burly woman, in some sort of
command at the place, was especially offended
at our audacity in thinking that we could see
Krishnamurti himself without a prior appoint-
ment. She was a proper lion! I thought she
actually had a point, although I wondered how
Krishnamurti would have responded to her
description of him when she growled at us,
"Anybody can walk in off the street and want
to see the high and the mighty!"

I knew we were not supposed to be
there, and I had not really expected to see
Krishnamurti; but I was like an iron filing naturally drawn by this magnet. I had not ana-
lyzed the situation and decided on a course of
action; it just had not occurred to me that I
could be within driving distance and not go to
meet him. While leaving, for some reason I
reached into my pocket and found a visiting
card which I gave to the lion to deliver to Mary
Zimbalist, who for the last many years had self-
lessly devoted herself to taking care of
Krishnamurti, often traveling with him. She
took the card from me with much hesitation,
and I was not sure she was going to deliver it;
but we tarried a little anyway. Soon I saw Mary

hurrying towards us, with a big smile. She greeted me and my friend most affectionately, explaining that things had been very hectic all morning: The BBC was filming a program on Krishnamurti, and a senior man from *The Times* of London was doing an interview. In any case, of course we must stay for lunch, and Krishna Ji would be along any minute now. Soon he appeared and welcomed us very warmly. At lunch, he looked fatigued and did not eat much. We spoke about this and that, and I wondered to myself how this man at such an advanced age could travel so much. What did he hope to accomplish? Could it be accomplished by talking to large numbers of people? Wasn't some sort of preparation required to make use of what he was saying? He said, "You should have been here in the morning; we had a wonderful discussion; a lot came out." I asked, "Can any real transformation take place just with discussion?" "No, sir," he said.

Krishnamurti's destiny was obviously to be a teacher, even though he tried strenuously to avoid being so labeled. He especially eschewed the devotional sort of adulation he received everywhere, particularly in India. After a public lecture in Madras, we went for a walk together. I wondered why he was trying to sneak out of the compound by a side door like a thief rather than walk out the main gate. "No, sir, they'll start touching my feet and all. Oh, God, no!" He had a special feeling for solitude. Even when walking with others he often preferred silence. We walked for a while in complete silence along the beach in Adyar. Suddenly he seemed to remember that I was in town with my children who went swimming there. "*Méfiez vous; faites attention!*" He knew I dabbled a bit in French; he particularly liked that and would occasionally say a few sentences to me in that language. He was warning me to make sure that my children realized that there was a strong undertow at that place and took proper precautions. I thanked him and wondered if he swam there himself. "I know this place well. You know this is where K was discovered by them!" he said conspiratorially.

I was supposed to meet him one evening in Ojai. When I arrived I found him working in the orange orchard pruning some trees. We stayed there a little while. He told me casually, "The speaker used to have healing powers, clairvoyance and all that. They have told me this; I don't know." He showed me the tree under which the "process" took place. He spoke very tenderly of his younger brother with whom he had lived in the cottage nearby. We stood there for a few minutes. He seemed to be actually seeing his brother there, and I think (I am not completely sure of this) he said that was the place where his brother had died. After a little while, I asked him, "What exactly is the 'process'?" I knew immediately that I had chosen a wrong moment to ask this. He looked at me sadly and said, "This is what everyone wants to know. Then they will start imitating it and faking it. No, it cannot be said."

I had often been struck by a similarity between the all-or-nothing absolutist stance of Krishnamurti and that of many Old Testament prophets. I was also sure that essentially, more than anything else, he was a lover at heart: a lover of nature, of presence, of truth and of silence. I was delighted and not at all surprised when he told me, in response to a question of mine, that his favorite book in the Bible was *The Song of Songs*. I told him that the great Rabbi Akiba had declared that book to be the holiest of the holies and that he had said that all the ages were not worth the day when this book was given to Israel. Krishnamurti was only mildly interested in Rabbi Akiba's comment about it but was delighted when I recalled a line: "I sleep, but my heart waketh: it is the voice of my beloved that knocketh. . . ."

I had been asked by the editors of an encyclopedia to write an article on Krishnamurti. I prepared the outline, made extensive notes, and had a special interview with him to make sure that what I had written accurately reflected his thought. I asked him whether "intelligence beyond thought" was the central thing that he spoke about. He agreed, but without much feeling. Suddenly, he was animated: "Take the risk, sir. Say what you wish. If you speak from the heart, I'll agree. Take the risk."

Once I was visiting Ojai, having promised Mary Zimbalist before coming there that I would not engage Krishna Ji in serious talk since he was taking a few days rest after a strenuous lecture series. In any case, I did not have anything specific to ask him; I simply wanted to be in his presence. I was in the kitchen talking to the cook when Krishnamurti entered by the side door on his way to lunch. He saw me and extended his hand with a broad smile. I took his hand and then hugged him. When he inquired after my wife and children, I gave him another hug from them. He was a little surprised, perhaps not being used to receiving physical affection. There were about a dozen people at lunch, talking about this and that. As lunch was ending, I said something about the subtle alchemical changes left in the body by an insight. Unexpectedly, he reached across the table, held my hand and said, "Sir, shall we go into it seriously?" "Some other time, Krishna Ji. Now it is time for you to have a rest," I said. He looked quite annoyed, as if we had no sense of the right priority of things. He insisted that we talk seriously there and then and asked for a tape recorder to be brought to record it. I looked at Mary to convey, "Look, it's not my fault. He is the one getting himself into it." She tried to suggest that we could talk later in the afternoon, but he would not hear of it.

So we had a serious conversation for a long time. At one point I said, "A new insight belongs to a new body, it seems to me. What do you think of that, Krishna Ji?" "You know, sir, it occurs to me that K does not think at all. That's strange. He just looks."

Once when I told him that he was a real scientist, a scientist of the interior, he seemed to like that. After a long silence, he said, "I have been going around the world talking for more than sixty years. Nobody under-stands what I am trying to say; especially the scientists. They are too clever for their own good." "You know, Krishna Ji, if they under-stood what you are saying, they wouldn't let you into the country. You are completely sub-versive." He laughed, "That's right, sir, don't tell them."

The last time I was in Ojai, it was as a guest of the Krotona Institute, where I had been invited to give a few lectures. Naturally, I went to see Krishnamurti as often as I could. He seemed to take a particularly mischievous de-light in the fact that the Theosophists were paying for me to come and see him. "Keep it up, sir. Don't tell them. Sneak out and come here as often as you can."

Since I had been so fascinated by the special nature and quality of Krishnamurti's mind, I often returned to that subject with him, and he would frequently speak about the reli-gious mind and its innocence, freshness and vulnerability. I was more interested in the par-ticularities of his mind. The more he tried to convince me to the contrary, the more I seemed to feel that Krishnamurti was in fact a freak. "What is the nature of your own mind, Krishna

Ji? What do you see when you look at that tree?" "My mind is like a mill-pond. Any disturbance that is created in it soon dies, leaving it unruffled as before," he said calmly. Then, as if reading what I was about to ask, he added with the most playful smile, "And your mind is like a mill!"

The last time I met him was in May, 1985, in Ojai, just before his ninetieth birthday. We had a long talk about death. During the conversation I had raised the same question which I had asked twenty years earlier. At the end he said,

> *The real question is "Can I die while I am living? Can I die to all my collections— material, psychological, religious?" If you can die to all that, then you'll find out what is there after death. Either there is nothing; absolutely nothing. Or there is something. But you cannot find out until you actually die while living. Don't accept it. No believing is necessary. Doubt it; question it.*

When I was leaving he came to the door and held it open. He looked a little frail, and I did not want him to stand there waiting while I put on my socks and shoes, which I had taken off at the entrance. My heart had been filled by what he had said, and I was taking my leave slowly. When I said again that he should go in and not wait there, he said, "The noble never close the door."

You don't need special training. What you need is to pay attention, not to what I say, but to your own mind.

Inquiry means a mind that is sane, healthy, that is not persuaded by opinions of its own or of another, so that is able to see very clearly, every minute, everything as it moves, as it flows. Life is a movement in relationship which is action. And unless there is freedom, mere revolt has no meaning at all. A really religious man is never in revolt. He is a free man—free, not from nationalism, greed, envy and all the rest of it; he is just free.

J. Krishnamurti

When you are inattentive, don't act. That requires a great deal of intelligence, a great deal of self-observation; because it's inattention that breeds mischief and misery.

When one gives one's heart, it is a total action. And when you give your mind, it is a fragmentary action. And most of us give our minds to so many things. That is why we live a fragmentary life—thinking one thing and doing another; and we are torn, contradictory. To understand something, one must give not only one's mind but one's heart to it.

J. Krishnamurti

SELECTED BIBLIOGRAPHY

There are many books by and about J. Krishnamurti. His own books are, in general, transcripts of the talks he gave at various places and to diverse groups. Many audio and video tapes of these talks are available from the Krishnamurti Foundation of America, Ojai, California. What follows is a representative selection of books about his life and thought.

Jayakar, Pupul and Sunanda Patwardhan (editors). *Within the Mind: On J. Krishnamurti*. Madras, India: Krishnamurti Foundation of India, 1982. (A collection of some articles about Krishnamurti's ideas, two of his talks and some discussions with him. There is a "Letter to J. Krishnamurti" by the present author in this collection.)

Jayakar, Pulpul. *Krishnamurti, A Biography*. New Delhi, India: Penguin Books, 1986. (Written by a long time devotee of Krishnamurti, this biography gives many details of Krishnamurti's visits in India, especially during 1947-49.)

Krishnamurti, Jiddu. *The Awakening of Intelligence*. New York: Harper & Row, 1973. (This volume contains several of Krishnamurti's talks, some small-group dialogues and some individual conversations with him.)

Krishnamurti, Jiddu. *Krishnamurti's Notebook*. New York: Harper & Row, 1976. (A record of Krishnamurti's perceptions and states of consciousness for a period of six months, commencing on June 18, 1961.)

Krishnamurti, Jiddu. *Krishnamurti to Himself—His Last Journal*. San Francisco: Harper & Row, 1987. (This is the written transcript of Krishnamurti's last journal, which he himself dictated into a tape recorder, revealing his concerns and his very keen observations of nature.)

Krishnamurti, Jiddu. *The Collected Works of J. Krishnamurti*. Kendall/Hunt Publications, 1991-92. (Many volumes are planned: at least seventeen have already been published, containing his talks and discussions from 1933 to 1967.)

Lutyens, Mary (editor). *The Penguin Krishnamurti Reader*.   Harmondsworth, Middlesex, England: Penguin Books, 1970. (A selection from three of Krishnamurti's books, namely, *The First and the Last Freedom, Life Ahead* and *This Matter of Culture*.)

Lutyens, Mary. *Krishnamurti: The Years of Awakening*. New York: Farrar, Straus and Giroux, 1975. (This is a biography of Krishnamurti from his birth in 1895 to the year 1933 when he completely broke away from the Theosophical Society. The author's mother, Lady Emily Lutyens, was Krishnamurti's chief confidante during most of this period, and many private letters Krishnamurti wrote to her are included in this volume.)

Lutyens, Mary. *Krishnamurti: The Years of Fulfillment*. NewYork: Farrar, Straus and Giroux, 1983. (This volume brings the story of Krishnamurti's life to 1980.)

Lutyens, Mary. *Krishnamurti: The Open Door*. New York: Farrar, Straus and Giroux, 1986. (This is the last volume in the biography, covering the period from 1980 to his death in February, 1986.)

Lutyens, Mary. *The Life and Death of Krishnamurti*. London, England: John Murray Publishers, 1990. (This volume is essentially a summary of all the biographical information about Krishnamurti contained in the above three books, with some additional material.)

Sloss, Radha Rajagopal. *Lives in the Shadow with J. Krishnamurti*. London, England: Bloomsbury, 1991. (This volume details a twenty-five year love affair between Krishnamurti and Rosalind Rajagopal, as witnessed, understood and interpreted by Rosalind's daughter, who grew up with Krishnamurti being very much a member of their household.)

Ravindra to Krishnamurti:

It is clear that a bridge cannot be built from here to There. But can it be built from There to here?

Krishnamurti to Ravindra:

Take the risk, sir. Say what you wish. If you speak from the heart, I'll agree. Take the risk.

Quest Books
are published by
The Theosophical Society in America,
Wheaton, Illinois 60189-0270,
a branch of a world organization
dedicated to the promotion of the unity of
humanity and the encouragement of the study of
religion, philosophy, and science, to the end that
we may better understand ourselves and our place
in the universe. The Society stands for complete
freedom of individual search and belief.
In the Classics Series well-known
theosophical works are made
available in popular editions.